Sports for Supergirls

D1737602

Aquatic Sports

Louise Spilsbury

Gareth Stevens
PUBLISHING

Please visit our website, **www.garethstevens.com**.
For a free color catalog of all our high-quality books,
call toll free 1-800-542-2595 or fax 1-877-542-2596.

Cataloging-in-Publication Data

Names: Spilsbury, Louise.
Title: Aquatic sports / Louise Spilsbury.
Description: New York : Gareth Stevens Publishing, 2020. | Series: Sports for supergirls
| Includes glossary and index.
Identifiers: ISBN 9781538242193 (pbk.) | ISBN 9781538241929 (library bound)
Subjects: LCSH: Aquatic sports--Juvenile literature. | Women athletes--Juvenile literature.
Classification: LCC GV770.5 S65 2020 | DDC 797--dc23

First Edition

Published in 2020 by
Gareth Stevens Publishing
111 East 14th Street, Suite 349
New York, NY 10003

© 2020 Gareth Stevens Publishing

Produced by Calcium
Editors: Sarah Eason and Jennifer Sanderson
Designers: Clare Webber and Jessica Moon

Photo credits: Cover: Shutterstock: YanLev; Inside: Wilfred Barbeau: p. 17b; Sage Donnelly: Stephanie Viselli:
p. 33; Shutterstock: ALPA PROD: p. 35; Big Joe: p. 30; Paolo Bona: p. 8l; Neale Cousland: p. 37t; CP DC Press:
p. 21b; Cultura Motion: p. 25b; Daniel_Dash: p. 42; Benoit Daoust: p. 14; Noah Densmore: p. 21t; Dontsov
Evgeny: p. 43; Geartooth Productions: p. 5b; Getmilitaryphotos: pp. 5t, 28; Mitch Gunn: p. 9; Christopher
Halloran: p. 17t; Jerry photo: p. 32; Joyfull: p. 25t; Kojin: p. 38; Kozlik: p. 34; LouisLotterPhotography: p. 23b,
26, 27t, 27b; Elina Manninen: p. 12; Valery V. Markov: p. 37b; Yana Mavlyutova: pp. 40, 41b; Dudarev Mikhail:
pp. 10, 11, 13t, 13b; Jaroslav Moravcik: p. 31; Ohrim: pp. 1, 6; KI Petro: p. 39t; Michel Piccaya: p. 16; Colin
Porteous: p. 20; PunkbarbyO: p. 19t; SAPhotog: p. 23t; Jose Ignacio Soto: p. 41t; Studio Peace: p. 7;
Sunnypicsoz: pp. 18, 19b; Jordan Tan: p. 39b; Tapat.p: p. 8br; Tunatura: p. 4; Wavebreakmedia: pp. 22, 24;
Jaren Jai Wicklund: pp. 3, 45; Daan Verhoeven: p. 15; Wikimedia Commons: Flying Cloud from Australia: p. 36;
James Heilman, MD: p. 29.

CPSIA compliance information: Batch #CS19GS:
For further information contact Gareth Stevens, New York, New York at 1-800-542-2595.

Contents

Chapter 1
Ruling the Waves!

Aquatic sports often involve adventure and sometimes danger, so they were once enjoyed mostly by men. Today, many women are taking up aquatic sports, too. They are diving and jumping into pools, seas, and lakes to join this exciting sporting world.

Most scuba divers get to 100 to 130 feet (30 to 40 m) below the surface, but the world record for the deepest scuba dive is 1,044 feet (318 m).

WHAT ARE AQUATIC SPORTS?

There are many different aquatic sports, from high diving and long-distance swimming to surfing and white-water rafting. The idea that these sports are for men only is a thing of the past. Aquatic sports require more than just brute strength: they need fitness and good technique and skills, so women are just as good at them as men. They are also great sports for keeping healthy and can lead to an exciting sports career.

POOL OR POND?

Aquatic sports are not only for those who live on the water's edge. Many aquatic sports are done in swimming pools or at aquatic centers, which can be outdoors or inside a building. These centers offer far more than a pool of water. Participants can take a range of classes, while some centers have wave machines that artificially generate waves across the water's surface.

FITNESS AND FUN

Often athletes' muscles ache for several days after taking part in aquatic sports. Many people find that water sports take more effort than land-based sports. Aquatic sports push against the force, or resistance, of the water, so they build muscle strength. As the body constantly moves against the water, pushing and pulling on it in different directions, participants become more flexible. Being in and around water is also relaxing, making aquatic sports great for relieving stress.

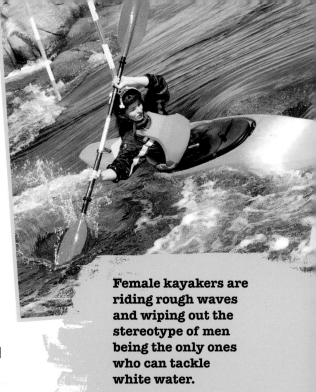

Female kayakers are riding rough waves and wiping out the stereotype of men being the only ones who can tackle white water.

GIRL TALK

Before trying any adventure water sport, participants need to be able to swim confidently. If they fall off water skis, stumble off a paddleboard, or slip off a sailboat, they need to know that they can swim to shore or keep afloat in the water until someone comes to get them.

Girls and women love the challenge and excitement of extreme aquatic sports.

Wild Waters

Aquatic sports are great for daring girls and women who are looking for water adventures and new experiences. Anyone wanting to try a new aquatic sport has a wide variety to choose from.

The best kite surfers can jump around 60 feet (18 m) high and can float for hundreds of feet when wind conditions are good.

KEEN ON KITE SURFING

Just like when people fly a kite in the air, kite surfing relies on the power of the wind, not an engine, to move the surfer along the water. Kite surfers stand on a board and use a large, steerable kite to drag themselves around an open area of water. Once a kite surfer has learned the basics, they can try all kinds of tricks.

Paddleboarding originated in Hawaii as an offshoot of surfing, but today, people all over the world are trying the sport.

PADDLEBOARDING

A stand-up paddleboard (SUP) can be great fun for riding wild waves or touring a coastline. Riders use balance and strength to stay upright on a large board while paddling. This sport is great for building core strength and works out nearly every muscle in the body.

GO WILD FOR WINDSURFING

Windsurfing, also called boardsailing, is a sport that combines elements of surfing and sailing. Athletes stand on a board that is usually 6.5 to 13 feet (2 to 4 m) long and ride quickly across the surface of the water, powered by the effect of the wind on a sail. Many people go windsurfing just for fun, while others compete in races of different kinds. Windsurfing has been an Olympic sport since 1984.

SCUBA DIVING

Every year, millions of people go scuba diving to explore the amazing colors and wildlife beneath the ocean surface. Scuba stands for Self-Contained Underwater Breathing Apparatus, and scuba divers carry equipment that allows them to breathe underwater so they can stay there for a long time.

GIRL TALK

Some fearless scuba divers go for a dive with sharks. A cage dive with sharks can be the experience of a lifetime. Scuba divers are enclosed inside a steel cage and lowered from a boat into a school of sharks.

Daring Divers

High diving can be dangerous, but women divers are among those who want to mix their love for the water with some action and excitement. There are different forms of diving, and each one demands different training and techniques. Each one also has its own challenges.

DIVING DOWN

High diving is the sport in which people plunge themselves into water headfirst, usually while performing acrobatics, such as somersaults and twists, midair. In competitions, divers leap from a platform or a springboard, typically set at different heights 10 to 33 feet (3 to 10 m) above the water's surface. In competitions, divers are judged on how well they accomplish the dive and how little splash they create on entering the water.

In synchronized diving, two divers must perform the save dive at exactly the same time.

Diving platforms are set at different heights above the water.

GIRL TALK

Diving off a proper diving board into a pool is fairly safe. Most diving accidents happen when people jump from structures such as bridges or piers into water that is not deep enough. People also get injured or even killed when they dive without realizing there are rocks or logs in the water below.

Case Study

JESSICA PARRATTO—BORN TO DIVE

Diving is in Jessica Parratto's blood. Jessica was born on June 26, 1994, to parents who were also divers. Her mother Amy was a five-time All-American diver at Wellesley College, Massachusetts. When Jessica started diving at four years old, her mother was her coach. She continued to coach Jessica until she was 14 years old.

LIVING HER DREAMS

In 2009, Jessica moved to Indiana to continue her training and schooling. Although she missed her home and family, the move led her to great things. She competed at the World Aquatics Championships in 2015, and in the Women's 10-meter (33-ft) platform at the 2016 Olympic Games in Rio de Janeiro, Brazil.

Before big competitions, Jessica follows the same routine. She has a large carbohydrate-filled dinner the night before and goes to bed early. She wakes early in the morning, takes a hot shower to loosen up, and then rides on a stationary bike to warm up her muscles.

When she is not training or competing, Jessica loves cooking and baking but also has fun doing outdoor adventure activities like hiking, camping, and rock climbing with friends. She enjoys pilates, which she recommends as a great way to stay strong.

US diver Jessica Parratto competes in a women's 10-meter (33-ft) competition in the United Kingdom in 2015.

Chapter 2
Free Diving

Many people dive into pools from a board or the poolside, holding their breath as they enter the water. Free divers take this kind of diving to another level. They train themselves to hold their breath so they can dive and swim down to incredible depths.

DEEP AND DARING

Some free divers are able to go more than 650 feet (200 m) underwater on a single breath. Some can hold their breath for an incredible 10 minutes. To be able to do this, they spend a long time learning underwater breath-holding techniques. They also learn how to relax, conserve oxygen, and restrict the flow of blood to their extremities in order to conserve oxygen for their vital organs.

DANGERS OF DIVING

Done correctly, free diving is exciting and exhilarating, and divers say there is nothing like the peace and calm they feel in deep, dark water. However, done incorrectly, free diving will lead to ear, nose, and lung damage, as well as decompression sickness, blacking out, and death.

Instead of carrying a tank of air like scuba divers, free divers have only the air in their lungs to keep them alive.

TYPES OF FREE DIVING

There are different types of free diving people do for fun and in competitions. There is free diving for time, distance, or depth. In competitions, divers in pools battle to see who can hold their breath the longest. Divers also compete to swim down as deep as possible on a single breath, with or without fins, or using a rope to pull them up and down. In one category, divers use a heavy sled to pull them downward. Many people consider the purest form of free diving to be when people swim down and up again without any help.

Free divers are the real daredevils of the diving world.

Safety First

Everyone who participates in free diving must be highly trained and follow strict safety rules, because there is always the risk that someone holds their breath for too long and cannot make it to the surface again. Anyone wishing to try free diving must know how to do it safely.

Free diving may look simple, but there is a lot that can go wrong, so it is important people learn what to do in a swimming pool before diving in the ocean.

GEAR UP

Deep water can be very cold, so divers wear wetsuits to keep warm. Masks allow them to see underwater. These need to fit comfortably and securely on the face and be made of special glass that will not break deep underwater where the water pressure is very strong. Fins should be long and flexible. Divers wear either one on each foot or a monofin, into which they put both feet. To go down deeper, trainee free divers typically use a weight belt or a rope to help them descend.

WISE UP!

Trainee free divers learn how to control their breathing, use their equipment correctly, and carefully prepare for the dive. Most classes start in the pool, where divers learn to take really deep breaths and control their breathing. They also learn how to swim with fins, which help them go to greater depths. Perfecting the best dive to get them down to depth is also important.

A coach teaches a free diver how to control their breathing in the shallow waters of a calm bay.

BUDDY UP

Free divers should never dive alone. They should always have a fully trained partner, known as their diving buddy, with them the entire time they are in the water. The buddy usually stays on the water's surface, often in a boat or sometimes in the water. A buddy watches over and monitors a diver at all times and is ready to help them if necessary.

GIRL TALK

Many free divers wear weight belts to prevent them from floating to the surface. These belts are attached to a line from the water's surface by a lanyard. Lanyards are an important safety device. If a diver gets into difficulty, the buddy travels down the line to find their lanyard and them.

Free divers train carefully and are confident in their skills before venturing into deep water.

The Deeper Blue

Interest in free diving has exploded in recent years. Free divers who go deep underwater without artificial breathing equipment describe it as a magical experience. They say that as a diver holds their breath and their heart rate starts to drop, everything around them seems to slow down and all they can hear is their heartbeat. All they can see is the deepest blue.

PUSHING TO THE LIMIT

Some free divers choose to compete to push their personal limits by holding their breath longer and diving deeper. There are free-diving competitions all around the world. Taking part in a free-diving event can be exciting and nerve-racking. For a start, there are certain rules divers have to follow. For example, when divers resurface, they should take off their mask and give a sign to the judge that they are all right. Failure to do so can lead to disqualification.

Athletes finish a free dive in competition by giving the "okay" hand sign to judges.

GIRL TALK

One skill the deepest divers must learn is how to equalize pressure underwater. Water exerts great pressure on the body and, the deeper divers go, the higher the pressure. The air spaces in the human body become smaller as the water pressure increases. Free divers seal their nose and blow out to add air to these spaces to equal out the pressure and keep safe.

MANDY SUMNER—WATER BABY

Mandy Sumner is a real water baby. She learned to swim before she could walk. Mandy grew up on the coast of southern Maine and started to take part in swimming competitions from the age of five. She began free diving in 2014, in Hawaii, and immediately loved the sport. She turned out to be a complete natural—within two months of starting lessons, Mandy entered her first international competition.

Since then, Mandy has traveled around the world to compete. In 2015, she became the first US free-diving athlete (male or female) to ever win a gold medal at an International Association for the Development of Apnea (AIDA) World Championship.

As a free-diving instructor and trainer, Mandy teaches people to free dive all over the world. This gives her a chance to share her passion for the beauty, love, safety, and respect of free diving and the world's deep blue oceans.

Mandy worked as a geologist, or rock expert, for 15 years before setting that aside to follow her passion for free diving.

Chapter 3
Sailing

For hundreds of years, oceangoing ships carried goods and passengers around the world using just the power of the wind pushing against their sails. Today, sailing is an exciting sport that thousands of people compete in.

Offshore sailing races are thrilling events and there are often thousands of spectators watching from the coastline.

SAILBOATS

All boats used for sailing races move forward without an engine. Sailing boats have sides, unlike the flat board used in windsurfing. There are two categories based on boat length. Small sailing boats with hulls up to around 20 feet (6 m) long are called dinghies. Longer sailing boats are called yachts.

GOING FASTER

Yachts generally have bigger sail areas than dinghies, so they trap more air and go faster. The biggest yachts have strong Kevlar sails, which are resistant to ripping. They also have tough, light masts.

Most yachts are called keelboats because they have a long, fixed blade, called a keel, sticking down from their single hull underwater. Keels help keep yachts from falling over, or capsizing, when they are moving fast. Catamarans are yachts with two hulls. The two hulls mean they are more stable at speed without a keel, which can drag underwater and slow them down.

The biggest racing yachts are over 80 feet (25 m) long and need crews of ten or more people to sail them at speeds of up to 50 miles per hour (81 km/h).

RACING

Racing a sailboat is exhilarating. Some races are over short distances on relatively calm inland reservoirs or lakes, with boats jostling for position against others nearby. Others are much longer events, covering parts of or whole oceans, battling some of the strongest winds and biggest waves. Some sailors race against the clock alone in their boats, but others are part of big teams working together.

GIRL TALK

Sailing solo across oceans is a dangerous activity. Tall ocean waves can crash on deck and wash sailors overboard. Boats can crash into floating objects such as containers from cargo ships. If sailors get sick or an accident happens, such as a broken mast, they may wait for days before they get help. Solo sailors need to be practical, prepared for emergencies, and calm under pressure.

Donna Lange from the United States sailed solo around the world twice, each voyage lasting more than eight months.

Learning the Ropes

Sailing is a physically demanding sport. It involves using strength and agility to change course and speed without taking an unwelcome dip in the water. Like many adventure sports, sailing can be risky for any sailor unless they learn the ropes.

SAILING SKILLS

Anyone can sail using a few important skills. Sail setting is changing the angle of the sail so the wind pushes the boat along in the direction the sailor wants to go. Following a chosen direction often requires tacking, or zigzagging, to use the wind when it is not blowing in the most helpful direction. Boat balance is another skill where sailors keep their boat from capsizing by distributing their weight (and that of other people in the boat) from side to side.

There is a variety of sailing classes and courses offered, many based at sailing clubs and marinas.

LINES OF DUTY

Any dinghy or yacht relies on pieces of rope or steel cable called lines. Some lines are always in place and hold masts upright. Others are movable. These lines raise, change the angle of, stretch, or loosen sails. Yet other lines are used to tie the boat to a dock. All sailors need to know how to tie knots to make the lines do their job and keep the boat and its passengers safe.

It is a fun challenge to learn the different knots required to do various jobs on a sailing boat.

SAFETY KIT

Sailors need to be prepared for the worst. They should wear shoes with good grip to avoid slipping on a wet boat, and gloves to pull on lines without losing grip or harming their palms, along with a buoyancy aid. Far out at sea, sailors need to have a radio set to call for help. They should also have flares so they can release them to be seen in the dark if the boat is in trouble.

Be prepared to duck the side-to-side movement of the boom, the beam that changes sail angle, when onboard a sailing boat!

GIRL TALK

A personal flotation device (PFD) is essential for any sailor, whether they are a beginner or competition standard. If a sailor is knocked overboard, the PFD will keep them afloat so they do not drown. PFDs come in different styles. Some are foam pull-on vests, which give protection if sailors fall from a boat at speed and bash into the water. Other PFDs are smaller, less visible harnesses that sailors inflate with gas from hidden cylinders if they fall in the water.

Sailing Class

The pinnacle of many competitive dinghy sailors' sporting lives is competing at the Olympic Games. Dinghies of the same class (with the same weight and sail size) compete against each other, so there is no unfair advantage for any crew. Crews try to outmaneuver each other and sail fastest around courses marked out in the water.

OLYMPIC RACES

The smallest Olympic dinghies are single-handed Lasers. The largest, with a crew of two, are double-hulled Nacras. The Finn class is still competed for by men only, but other classes have separate women's and men's races, except Nacra-class catamarans, which have mixed crews.

There was a dramatic race to the finish line in the women's pair sailing event of the London Olympics in 2012.

ERIKA REINEKE—LASER INSPIRATION

Erika Reineke started sailing when she was just eight years old. She began competing in fun races in Optimist dinghies and, by the age of 12, was winning junior titles. Her coaches spotted an exceptional talent and, with their help and Erika's determination, she was soon the US girls' national champion.

Inspired by a talk by Anna Tunnicliffe, Laser Olympic gold medalist, Erika decided to make sailing her career. In her later teens, she shifted to the larger and faster Laser Radial boats and, within a couple of years, she was competing internationally. By 2012, aged 18, she had won three youth world championships.

Her success continued once she went to Boston College, where she not only won several singlehanded national championships and Women's Sailor of the Year awards, but also graduated with a degree in science. Reineke is now training full time for her next goal: Laser Radial gold at the 2020 Olympics in Tokyo, Japan.

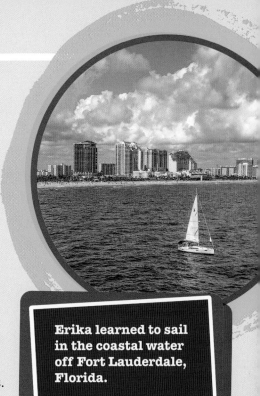

Erika learned to sail in the coastal water off Fort Lauderdale, Florida.

GIRL TALK

Sailors of fast, light dinghies, such as Lasers and 49ers, need to be prepared for the death roll. This is wind from behind a moving boat, which makes the sail swing around on its pole so its weight pulls over the boat, dunking the sailors in the water. Sailors need to then stand on the upper edge of the boat, holding onto ropes and using their body weight to get it upright again.

Laser races are fast, close, and fiercely fought competitions.

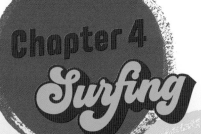

Chapter 4
Surfing

Surfers cannot get enough of the feeling of gliding across the water on a board with the wind blowing through their hair. They say surfing feels like flying, skating, swimming, and walking on water all in one! Surfing is challenging and exhilarating, and more and more women around the world are heading out to sea to try to catch ever-bigger waves.

Surfers paddle out to sea to find the biggest and best waves for riding.

CATCHING A WAVE

The best surfers know how to catch a wave at just the right moment. Waves break when the top of the wave falls over. When they see a wave coming, surfers get into position as near to the peak of the wave as possible, and then they paddle as fast as they can. They aim to catch a wave in the place where the wave is steepest, but not yet curled over and breaking.

The bigger the waves a surfer tries to ride, the bigger the chances that they will wipe out!

GIRL TALK

A bad wipeout can lead to injuries, collisions, broken boards, or worse. Most wipeout injuries happen because a surfer is hit by their own board. That is why surfers try to fall off on the ocean side of their board. They do not want be in the sea between the beach and the board, where there is a risk of a wave smashing the board into them.

WIPEOUT!

Even the best surfers wipe out, or get thrown off their board, now and then. This can happen if they catch a wave just as it is breaking because this can cause the surfboard to nosedive. As soon as a surfer realizes they are going to wipe out, they jump away from the board toward the ocean, not the beach. They try to fall to the side or to the back of the board, covering their head with their arms as they fall.

SURF AWAY THE STRESS

Surfing gives the body a great workout. It is also good for the mind. As well as helping participants to develop a strong core, shoulders, and back, many people find that being in the sea and riding the waves helps reduce any stress they are feeling. Surfing does this because exercise encourages the body to release endorphins, which are chemicals that can help a person feel good.

Surfers estimate where a wave is going to break and get into a good place to catch it.

Riding the Waves

Anyone who is interested in learning to surf needs to practice the skills needed and to have the right equipment. Surfing is a far more complex sport than it looks, so it is best to learn the basic techniques from qualified instructors.

GETTING BOARD?

First-timers should rent a surfboard if they have never tried surfing before. There are rental shops at most major surfing beaches, which hire out boards by the hour or day. Staff there should be able to help newcomers, or newbies, choose the correct type of surfboard for their size and weight. Most newbies start with soft boards that float well and are strong. A leash goes around the surfer's ankle, so boards do not become separated from their rider and smash into rocks or other surfers.

Leashes keep surfers from being stranded without a surfboard if they wipe out.

STARTING OUT

New surfers do not start in the sea; instead, they start on the sand. They lie straight down the middle of their board and practice paddling both arms, to get out to sea. Next they work on the tricky art of standing up on the board while on the water by pushing the body up with the arms and tucking the feet into position. Then they learn how to stand on the board at sea: with knees bent, arms loose and extended, feet firmly planted on the board, and their upper body leaning forward to lower their center of gravity. When surfers catch their first wave, they need to keep their eyes focused on where they are going and let the wave carry them in to shore.

Surfers should take lessons where they can learn surfing basics on the beach before taking to the water.

GIRL TALK

Surfing can be dangerous if people are not careful. Crashes between surfboards and other surfers can cause serious injuries, so it is important that surfers are aware of others in the water at all times.

SURFING SAFETY

There are certain things every surfer should do to remain safe:

• Go with a buddy: Surfers must look out for one another, especially when the waves are big.

• Tell someone when and where they are going surfing and when they expect to return.

• Check the weather forecast and the tides before setting out.

• Do not try to tackle waves bigger than they know they can cope with.

• Stay within lifeguarded areas of water, in case they run into trouble.

Surfers wax their boards to give them better grip when riding the waves.

Surfing Stars

The tricks and twists that the most talented surfing stars perform are amazing and draw big crowds to beaches the world over. After several decades of fighting to have surfing included, this aquatic sport will make its Olympic debut with 20 men and 20 women competing at the 2020 Olympic Games.

WINNING SCORES

Surfers can enter competitions for fun, prizes, medals, or money. Judges award marks for the different elements of a surfer's ride, such as how difficult it is, what maneuvers the surfer does, what combination and variety of tricks they do, and their speed.

GIRL TALK

Some competitions have been canceled due to sharks swimming in the area. Shark attacks are rare, but sharks have sometimes mistaken unfortunate surfers for prey animals and given them nasty bites and injuries.

US surfer "Lakey" Peterson (left) and Australia's Stephanie Gilmore hold their shields on the podium during the World Surf League Championship in 2018.

Case Study

LAURA LOUISE PETERSON— THE LAKEY LEGEND

Laura Louise "Lakey" Peterson is not your average surfer girl. As a professional surfer, she won the 2012 US Open of Surf and was ranked the Number 1 women's surfer in the world after winning the 2018 World Surf League Roxy Pro.

So how did Peterson get to where she is today? Peterson was born on September 30, 1994, and discovered surfing when she was just five years old, when her parents took her and her two older siblings on a long trip around the world. While they were staying in Australia, she earned the nickname "Lakey Legend" from locals impressed by her ability to catch wave after wave on her board.

Back home in the United States, Lakey tried tennis, football, baseball, and basketball, but ultimately returned to surfing. By the time she was 12 years old, she had started competing. At the age of 14, she won the National Scholastic Surfing Association (NSSA) Open Women's Title, in which she became the first female surfer to perform an aerial maneuver in competition.

Since then, Lakey has traveled all over the world and has even starred in a documentary about her life. She made *Zero to 100* because there were no female surf movies, but tons of surf films featuring men. She hopes to show other girls that hard work eventually pays off and to tell them not to settle for good—be great!

> Before competitions, Laura Louise prepares with breathing exercises to keep her focused.

Chapter 5
White-water Kayaking

White-water kayaking is not for the fainthearted! It takes nerves of steel to raft over rough waters, battling the swirling waves and attempting to stay upright as the water tries to capsize the kayak.

Kayakers exercise their upper body muscles to ensure they can paddle hard on the water.

KAYAKING IN WHITE WATER

White-water kayaking is the sport of paddling a kayak on a moving body of water, typically a white-water river. What makes this sport such a challenge is the type of water on which paddlers kayak. White water is turbulent water that flows over rapids, which are sections of a river where the river is narrow and steep and the water moves very fast, often over rocks. As the water gets churned up, it becomes frothy and bubbly, which is why it looks white.

HOW IT WORKS

Experienced kayakers sit up straight in their kayak and control their upper and lower body to keep balanced. When they paddle, they keep their arms stiff and straight, using the larger muscles in their chest, back, and stomach to move the paddle. They know how to use a variety of different strokes for every direction their kayak can travel. Their bent knees point outward and touch the kayak to help balance the boat, but kayakers can also push with their knees or lift a knee to direct their kayak.

GOING OVER WATERFALLS

On an outdoor kayak run, people also tackle waterfalls along a river. In white-water kayaking lingo, "huck" means kayaking over a waterfall. "Boofing" means raising the front of the kayak as the paddler falls over the waterfall ledge. This keeps the front of the kayak from diving straight into the water by ensuring it lands flat when it hits the water at the bottom of the waterfall.

GIRL TALK

The International Scale of River Difficulty is the US version of a rating system used to compare river difficulty throughout the world. In it, white-water rivers are graded from one to six, where one is a calm, easy, slow, and perfectly safe river, while six is a dangerous, furious, fast river that is almost impossible, even for an expert, to tackle.

A kayaker must paddle hard to get through white water without capsizing.

Paddle Hard

Anyone who wants to take up white-water kayaking and challenge the raw power of nature in a river of wild water needs to learn the basics. This sport is extreme and people cannot just get into a kayak and set off down a river. First, they must practice basic kayaking skills in the safety of an area of calm water, a swimming pool, or an aquatic center.

Once a kayaker becomes skilled enough, they can begin to kayak in open water.

BACK TO BASICS

A beginner kayaker's first task is to learn how to get in and sit properly in their kayak. Then they learn how to hold and use the paddle, which should be propelled by the torso and not the arms. The idea is to rotate the body while extending and retracting the arms. After this, a kayaker is ready to learn how to paddle forward, how to stop by pushing the back side of the paddle into the water, and other maneuvers.

ON A ROLL

Every kayaker will capsize someday, so they must learn how to flip their boat upright after capsizing. When a kayak is upside down, the paddle must be brought up near the surface to grab the water. Then the kayaker throws their hips to the right and then to the left, almost as if they are wiggling in their seat. This creates the momentum needed to roll the kayak upright.

Learning to turn a capsized kayak upright again is an essential skill.

KAYAKING GEAR

White water is cold and dangerous, so kayakers must be prepared and have all the equipment they need. They must always wear a helmet to protect them from hitting their head on rocks if they fall out of their boat. If they do fall out, their buoyancy aid will also help them keep afloat. Most kayakers wear drysuits. These look like wetsuits but they offer more waterproof protection. Gloves protect their hands and help kayakers grip a paddle tightly, and boots are also essential. Boots should be waterproof, padded, and have a good sole that can walk over rough rocks.

GIRL TALK

The most important things to learn when white-water kayaking are river safety and how to "read" the river. Kayakers must be able to identify suitable routes through complex rapids and spot potential hazards. They should also learn to look out for other kayakers and how to rescue them if they get into difficulties.

Racing the Rapids

Many white-water kayakers just love racing rapids out in the wild, but others also take part in competitions to test their skills against other devotees of the sport. Slalom is a major competitive form of kayaking and is the only white-water event in the Olympic Games. For the Olympics, special white-water stadiums are built, where the speed of the water and the height and difficulty of the rapids can be controlled.

HOW RACES WORK

In a slalom event, kayakers must speed from the top to the bottom of a section of river or white-water stadium as fast as possible, while correctly negotiating a series of gates. The gates are double poles suspended vertically over the river. There are usually 18 to 25 gates in a race, and kayakers must pass through them in the correct order. For example, they must go down through green gates and up through red gates, paddling furiously against the current.

GIRL TALK

Olympic white-water slalom events are dynamic and very challenging. Competitors have no idea where the gates' final positions will be for the competition because the current is very strong and a course can completely change between rounds.

In the Olympic slalom event, racers try to maneuver through a series of gates the fastest. Hitting a gate in an Olympic slalom white-water event costs competitors vital points.

Case Study

SAGE DONNELLY— SPORTING SUPERGIRL

Sage Donnelly is fast becoming one of the top US kayakers in spite of battling not one but three health issues. Her sights are firmly set on competing in the slalom competition at the 2020 Olympics in Tokyo, Japan.

Sage was diagnosed with Type 1 diabetes when she was three years old, celiac disease (an illness that affects the lining of the gut) at age eight, and thyroid disease at age eleven. Sage has to constantly watch what she eats, monitor her blood sugar levels, and take medication for her thyroid disease, but none of this holds her back. She says that while diabetes makes life harder, she will not let it keep her from doing what she loves.

Sage competes at kayaking events around the world and, in 2018, won the USA Freestyle National Championships in Columbus, Georgia, by wowing the judge with an amazing trick called a helix. In this trick off a wave, she did a 270-degree spin, during at least 180 degrees of which her boat was upside down and in the air!

Sage Donnelly, a rising star in the world of kayaking, is unstoppable when it comes to competing in slalom and downriver races.

Chapter 6
Waterskiing and Wakeboarding

Not many people have what it takes to be towed along at high speeds behind a motorboat while balancing on waterskis or a wakeboard. To enjoy the thrills and spills of tow sports, people need not only bravery, but also strong muscles and good balance, or they will spend more time in the water than on it.

SKIING ON WATER

When participants strap on a pair of waterskis, they have to be ready for the ride of their life! Skiers lean slightly backward while holding onto a handle on a rope attached to the rear of a speedboat. The boat tows them along at speeds of more than 15 miles per hour (24 km/h).

Balance is crucial on waterskis. If participants lean too far back, they will fall over backward, but too far forward, and they will end up flat on their face.

BE STRONG

Core strength is a waterskier's main weapon. When the muscles of the torso are strong, they help hold the body straight and stable, and allow the arms and legs to move with power. Waterskiers also need a wetsuit to keep them dry and warm, and a buoyancy aid for when the inevitable happens and they end up in the water.

GIRL TALK

Tow sports like skiing are great fun but they can be dangerous. People can fall in the water, collide with other skiers or objects, get hit by the boat pulling them, or get tangled in tow lines. Beginners should ski only in enclosed, calm areas of water where there are no other users nearby.

HOW TO WATERSKI

Those who are new to waterskiing start in the water with their knees bent up to their chest, arms held straight and outside the knees. As the boat sets off and the rope starts to pull, they must keep their arms straight and slowly start to stand, all the time keeping their shoulders level and the rope between their skis. Once they are standing on their ski blades, their head should be directly over their feet and they should keep looking ahead. Glancing down at their waterskis will unbalance them and they will fall in the water.

Making sure they have the right equipment and know how to use it is vital for all new waterskiers.

Blades on the Water

Some people ski just for fun with friends at weekends and during vacations. Others train to take part in competitions. In waterskiing contests, athletes are expected to do more than ride along behind a boat.

Show skiers are graceful as they perform ballet and other dance displays on their skis.

FAST TRICKS!

There are different kinds of skiing contests. Speed skiing lives up to its name as it pits waterskiers in fast races against each other, often side by side. Trick waterskiing competitions include tricks and jumps off ramps, sometimes performed on a single waterski rather than two skis. In show skiing, athletes do acrobatics and dance on waterskis to music. Slalom waterskiers zigzag back and forth between a set of buoys. Barefoot skiing is just what it sounds like: athletes wear water shoes but do not use skis to do tricks behind their boat.

REGINA JAQUESS— SLALOM STAR

Regina Jaquess is a seven-time world champion who skis for the US Water Ski team. Regina has been named USA Water Ski Athlete of the Year eight times since first earning the honor in 2001.

Regina was born on June 7, 1984, in Duluth, Georgia. She began skiing before her third birthday and was such a natural that she began competing in waterski events when she was just five years old. Since then, she has racked up medals, records, and wins time and time again. One of her best jumps is 176 feet (54 m) and, in 2016, she set a new women's world record for waterski slalom.

Regina Jaquess takes to the water in a slalom event, showing spectators just how it is done.

The number of talented female waterskiers is on the rise.

What is amazing about Regina is that she does all this while running her own pharmacy in Santa Rosa Beach, Florida. On an average day, she wakes up at sunrise and trains, then works at the pharmacy. She sneaks in a lunchtime session if she can, then trains after work in the evening, too.

GIRL TALK

In waterskiing, as in some other sports, women do not get paid the same as their male equals. Regina Jaquess is on record as saying that, for most professional events, the cash prize is higher for men than women. Thankfully, this is changing as more women get involved and demand equality.

Born to Board

Wakeboarding is an awesome way to have thrills and fun on the water. This tow sport combines elements of surfing, waterskiing, and snowboarding, and all of the excitement of those three sports. Wakeboarders stand on a board and perform tricks or ride the waves traveling at high speed, usually towed behind a motorboat.

Cable wakeboarders are daring supergirls who complete obstacle courses while keeping on their wakeboard.

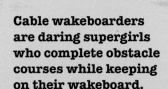

TYPES OF WAKEBOARDING

There are two main types of wakeboarding. The traditional version of the sport involves being towed by a boat, just like with waterskiing. The wake, or waves created by the boat, offers the kick off that athletes need to get their jumps. Cable wakeboarding involves holding onto a rope attached to a cable mechanism, which takes riders around a circuit, often laid out with ramps and other obstacles.

READY TO RIDE

Wakeboarding is fairly easy to learn. First, however, new wakeboarders need to get the right equipment. There are different boards for different weights and skill levels. Fins on the underside of the board enable it to be maneuvered more easily. Boots, or bindings, hook onto the wakeboard to hold riders in place. All riders must wear a buoyancy aid. This keeps them afloat while they wait to get towed, and also protects them from bumps and bruises. Wakeboarders also wear wetsuits to keep them dry and warm, and helmets to protect their head.

Wakeboarders can zip along at speeds of 18 to 25 miles per hour (30 to 40 km/h).

LEARNING TO WAKEBOARD

Longer wakeboards are easier to control for new riders. Using a shorter rope can also make a huge difference when riders are first learning, because they do not blow around too much. Most people practice the basics, like how to stand on a board, on land. Then they learn to stand up in water and how to steer. Steering is done by pushing down with their heels or toes, depending on what direction they want to go.

Once they get up, wakeboarders keep most of their weight balanced on their back leg as they ride.

GIRL TALK

Wakeboarders and waterskiers need a motorboat driver and a spotter. A spotter is someone on the boat who keeps an eye on things while people are being towed. Wakeboarders and spotters communicate using hand signals. Thumbs up means go faster. If a rider does a slashing motion across their neck, the driver should stop immediately.

Big Air, Big Tricks

Some people wakeboard just for fun, but other wakeboarders take it to a whole new level. They wow competition audiences with tricks and flips high into the air. Getting air is the name of the game! The higher the jump they perform, the more air they have. To get more lift and more air, the best wakeboarders jump off the very top of the wake.

GIRL TALK

Andrea Gaytan is a four-time world champion wakeboarder and the first woman in the world who managed to successfully perform a krypt on her wakeboard. A krypt is a handstand in the air followed by landing upright on the water.

Wakeboard jumps are performed by hitting the wake and launching into the air.

ROLLS AND FLIPS

Talented wakeboarders do variations of the two most basic and popular jumps: the roll and the flip. A roll is when a wakeboarder takes the wakeboard over their head, turning sideways, landing in the same direction in which they started. When they flip, they move the tail end of the board over the tip or front.

Competitions inspire wakeboarders to practice and try ever more daring tricks. They do amazing acrobatics such as a double front roll, called the speedball or the whirlybird, which is a back roll with a full 360-degree spin. A 720 is when wakeboarders jump up high and turn a full 720 degrees, or two complete circles, in the air before they land on the water again!

Case Study

LARISA MORALES— THE GIRL WHO WALKS ON WATER

Larisa Morales earned herself the nickname "the girl who walks on water" through talent, sheer hard work, and determination. Today, she is a top wakeboarder and constantly experiments with new tricks and maneuvers.

Larisa was born on July 9, 1997, in Monterrey, Mexico. She fell in love with wakeboarding at the age of six during family weekend trips to a lake—and she has been collecting trophies ever since. She has even taken part in a photoshoot where she was lowered into incredible cenotes (natural underground reservoirs) in Mexico to wakeboard through rocky water inhabited by crocodiles!

Larissa was the first Mexican female wakeboarder to successfully land a 720.

Larisa went wakeboarding in a Mexican cenote like this one.

Experienced wakeboarders use shorter boards because it is easier to spin and perform tricks as they flip or jump across the wake.

Becoming a Supergirl

In the past, girls and women were deterred from participating in the more extreme aquatic sports because the sports had a reputation for being dangerous and for men only. Nowadays, the water is filled with adventurous women trying and loving these wild water sports.

GIRL POWER

Sporting supergirls are not just those who make it to the top of their game and win medals at the Olympic Games and other international competitions. Learning to waterski, wakeboard, free dive, or any of these aquatic adventure sports, will give you confidence, strength, fitness, and a determination to succeed in all walks of life, and those are the characteristics that make a true supergirl. Many supergirls simply enjoy doing aquatic sports as a hobby or a regular workout and appreciate the chance to make some new friends.

Whether you do your chosen aquatic sport for fun or to win, get out there and enjoy life on the waves!

GIVE IT A GO!

Some sporting supergirls decide that they do want to take it to the next level by starting to enter competitions. This will take time and effort. It is good to start young as this gives you more time to hone your skills. If you want to win medals, you will have to be prepared to give up a lot of your free time to train. You may have to be at the pool or in the lake or sea before and after school. Winning takes dedication and determination.

AQUATIC SPORT CAREERS

If you are good with people, you might want to try a career such as being an instructor, mentor, or coach of aquatic sports. Teaching water sports is different from teaching sports on dry land. As well as improving people's skills in their chosen sport, trainers must also develop their confidence to do the sport in or on the water, especially if they have never been active on the water before. Other aquatic sports careers include organizing events, championships, and games, promoting competitions to tell people about them, or writing reports and reviews about athletes or events.

One of the great things about being a surf or other aquatic sports instructor is that you get to work in some of the world's most beautiful outdoor spaces.

GIRL TALK

Watersport athletes should be the biggest warriors in protecting oceans and lakes from pollution. They should take care not to drive speedboats too near wildlife and to ensure they do not leave plastic waste or other litter on beaches or in the water.

Try It Out!

Find out just how great girls can be at all kinds of aquatic sports—then find your inner supergirl and try them out for yourself! There are so many sports to choose from that there is sure to be one that appeals to you.

Regardless of what sport you want to try, whether it is surfing, waterskiing, or diving, there are pools and aquatic centers around the United States where you can learn some new skills.

HIGH DIVING

If you have a head for heights and would like to try high diving, find a coach at:
https://swimmingcoach.org

FREE DIVING

No one should attempt free diving without completing a course of lessons. The United States Freediving Federation will be able to put you in touch with an instructor near you. Contact the Freediving Federation at:
https://usfreedivingfederation.org/joinus

YACHT RACING

Boating is a great sport because you can sail solo or as part of a crew. Find a boating course near you at:
http://cgaux.org/boatinged

Find a certified sailing instructor near you at:
https://americasboatingclub.org/education-matters/in-person-boating-education

SURFING

If riding the waves and being in the ocean is your thing, log on to find a surf school at:
www.boardcave.com/surf-schools/usa

WHITE-WATER KAYAKING

White-water kayaking can be very dangerous so it is always advised to sign up for a course. To find white-water kayak courses near you, type "white water kayak lessons in <insert region where you live>" into your Internet search engine.

WATERSKIING

Find out about junior waterskiing opportunities at:
www.usawaterski.org/pages/divisions/3event/
JuniorDevelopmentProfile.htm

Click on "Regional Web Sites" in the menu to find a waterski club in your area.

WAKEBOARDING

Connect with a USA Water Ski & Wakeboard Sports affiliated club near you via:
www.sharelifeonthewater.com/basic-skills.html

There are many clubs where newbies find their feet and learn how to kayak safely and skillfully.

Glossary

aquatic related to water

buoyancy aid a sleeveless padded jacket that helps people float

capsizing turning upside down in the water

center of gravity the point in an object where its weight is balanced

conserve to keep in a sound or safe state

core the muscles within the torso

current water flowing in a particular direction

decompression sickness a serious condition caused by coming up from a deep dive too fast, due to the change in water pressure

diabetes a serious, lifelong condition where a person's blood sugars are too high

endorphins chemicals naturally released in the brain that can make you feel relaxed or full of energy

extremities the end parts of the limbs, such as hands and feet

flares devices that release a blaze of light to attract attention

hull the main body of a ship or boat

Kevlar a heat-resistant and very strong man-made fiber

lanyard a cord or strap for holding something in place

lift the force that directly opposes the weight of an object and holds it in the air

mast a tall upright post on a boat or ship that supports its sails

mentor a person who gives someone younger or less experienced help and advice over a period of time

momentum the force that keeps an object moving or keeps an event developing after it has started

pilates a form of exercise that is typically done on a floor mat and aims to strengthen the muscles, especially in the torso

pressure pushing force

reservoirs man-made lakes

resistance the force water (or air) exerts against a moving object that slows it down

thyroid a small gland in the neck that affects growth

torso the trunk or central part of the body that does not include the head, arms, or legs

vital organs the main organs inside the body, such as the heart, lungs, and brain, that are necessary for life

wake the waves made by a boat as it cuts through the water

wetsuits close-fitting suits made of material such as neoprene that keep people warm in cold water

wipeout a fall from a surfboard

BOOKS

Buckley, Jim. *Big Wave Surfing* (Intense Sports). Vero Beach, FL: Rourke Educational Media, 2018.

Butler, Erin K. *Extreme Water Sports* (Sports to the Extreme). North Mankato, MN: Edge Books, 2017.

Hamilton, Bethany. *Be Unstoppable: The Art of Never Giving Up*. Grand Rapids, MI: Zondervan, 2018.

Sherman, Jill. *Racing Personal Watercraft (Sea-Doos)* (Speed Racers). New York, NY: Enslow Publishing, 2018.

Walsh, Jenni L. *Bethany Hamilton* (She Dared). New York, NY: Scholastic, 2019.

WEBSITES

Learn more boating know-how at:
https://americasboatingclub.org/education-matters/online-boating-education

Check the weather at sea before you go out at:
www.nws.noaa.gov/om/marine/home.htm

Learn more about water safety at:
www.redcross.org/content/dam/redcross/atg/PDF_s/SwimmingWaterSafety.pdf

Learn to be safe in a kayak at:
http://rentalboatsafety.com/canoe-kayak.php